Contents

Any words appearing in the text in bold, **like this**,
are explained in the Glossary.

What is colour?

Colour is something you see when you look at an object. These flowers are pink and yellow. The butterfly is orange, black and white.

SCHOOLS LIBRARY SERVICE
MALTBY LIBRARY HEADQUARTERS
HIGH STREET
MALTBY
ROTHERHAM
S66 8LD

DEC 2002

MSC

ROTHERHAM LIBRARY & INFORMATION SERVICES

This book must be returned by the date specified at the time of issue
as the DATE DUE FOR RETURN.
The loan may be extended (personally, by post or telephone) for a
further period if the book is not required by another reader, by quoting
the above number / author / title.

LIS7a

www.heinemann.co.uk/library
Visit our website to find out more information about **Heinemann Library** books.

To order:
☎ Phone 44 (0) 1865 888066
▤ Send a fax to 44 (0) 1865 314091
▯ Visit the Heinemann Bookshop at www.heinemann.co.uk/library to browse our catalogue and order online.

First published in Great Britain by Heinemann Library, Halley Court, Jordan Hill, Oxford, OX2 8EJ, a division of Reed Educational & Professional Publishing Ltd. Heinemann is a registered trademark of Reed Educational & Professional Publishing Ltd.

OXFORD   MELBOURNE   AUCKLAND   JOHANNESBURG   BLANTYRE
GABORONE   IBADAN   PORTSMOUTH NH (USA)   CHICAGO

© Reed Educational and Professional Publishing Ltd 2001
The moral right of the proprietor has been asserted.

All rights reserved. No part of this publication may be reproduced, stored in a retrieval system, or transmitted in any form or by any means, electronic, mechanical, photocopying, recording, or otherwise without either the prior written permission of the Publishers or a licence permitting restricted copying in the United Kingdom issued by the Copyright Licensing Agency Ltd, 90 Tottenham Court Road, London W1P 0LP.

Designed by bigtop, Bicester, UK
Originated by Ambassador Litho Ltd.
Printed and bound in Hong Kong/China

06 05 04 03 02
10 9 8 7 6 5 4 3 2

06 05 04 03 02
10 9 8 7 6 5 4 3 2

ISBN 0 431 13713 7 (hardback)

ISBN 0 431 13719 6 (paperback)

British Library Cataloguing in Publication Data
Royston, Angela
Colour. - (My world of science)
1. Color - Juvenile literature   2. Colors - Juvenile literature
I. Title
535.6

ROTHERHAM LIBRARY &
INFORMATION SERVICES

B48 080193 2

Askews

J535.6 | £5.50

R0/003 7264

Acknowledgements
The Publishers would like to thank the following for permission to reproduce photographs:
Collections: Brian Shuel p23; Corbis: pp4, 6, 13, 17, 28; Stone: pp7, 12; Trevor Clifford: pp8, 9, 10, 11, 14, 15, 16, 18, 19, 20, 21, 22, 24, 25, 26, 27; Trip: G Harris p29, H Rogers p5.

Cover photograph reproduced with permission of Stone.

Every effort has been made to contact copyright holders of any material reproduced in this book. Any omissions will be rectified in subsequent printings if notice is given to the Publisher.

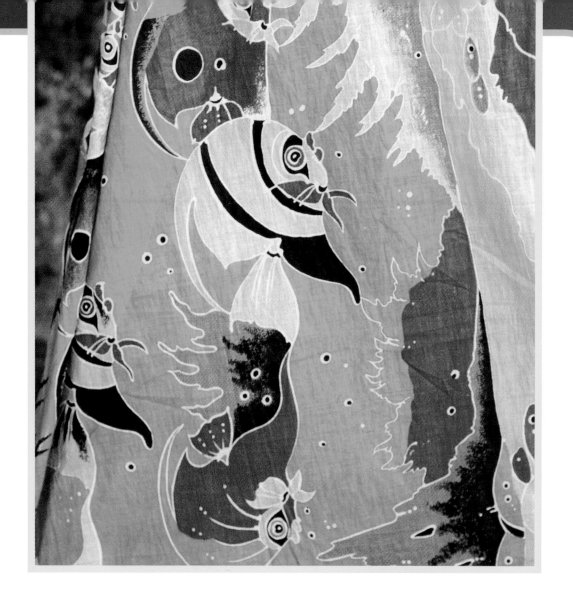

Some things are all one colour. Others have different colours in them. How many different colours can you see in this piece of cloth?

Colours as signs

Some colours are used as signs. Traffic lights help traffic move smoothly and safely. The red light means stop. The green light means go.

These basketball players are in two teams. Each team wears a specially coloured shirt. This is so everyone can tell one team from the other.

Paints and dyes

Artists often use paints to make different colours in their pictures. Paint is a **pigment**. Crayons, coloured pencils, pens and **dyes** all contain pigments too.

Cloth can be coloured using a dye. The dye soaks into the cloth and changes its colour. This T-shirt used to be all white!

Primary colours

Red, blue and yellow are called **primary colours**. They cannot be made from any other colours of paint.

Red is a bright, cheerful colour. This girl is wearing a red jumper. What other red things is she wearing?

Yellow and blue

Yellow is so bright it stands out from other colours. These workers are checking **waste**. They wear yellow clothes so other workers can see them easily.

The sea and the sky are often bright blue. Sometimes the sea and sky are grey. But the sea is always coloured blue on a map.

Mixing paints

Red, blue and yellow paints are mixed together to make other colours. Red and blue mixed together make purple. Red mixed with yellow makes orange.

When blue and yellow paints are mixed, they make green. Red, blue and yellow mixed together make brown.

Black and white

Black is a strong colour. This boy is using **charcoal** to draw in black. Black is the colour of night, when there is no light.

White is the lightest colour. This
building is made of white stone.
It shines in bright sunshine.

Shades of colour

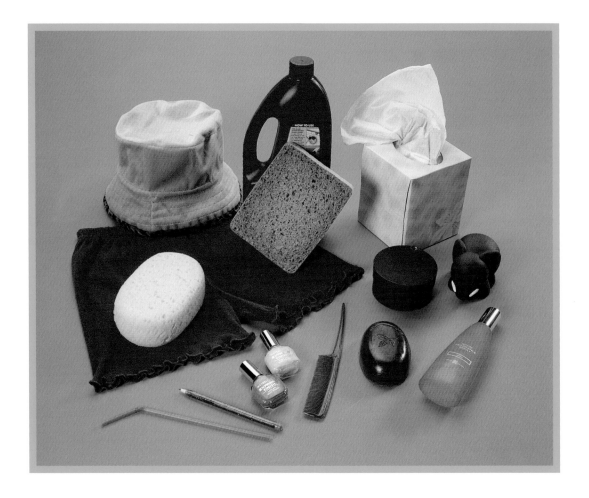

White is used to make many shades of colour. Adding white to red gives pink. Which two things are the palest pink? They are the ones with the most white.

One colour shades into another.
Turquoise is a mixture of blue and
green. The candle is turquoise. Mauve
is a mixture of red and purple.

Printing pictures

The pictures in a book use just four colours of ink – red, yellow, blue and black. Small dots of these colours make up the other colours.

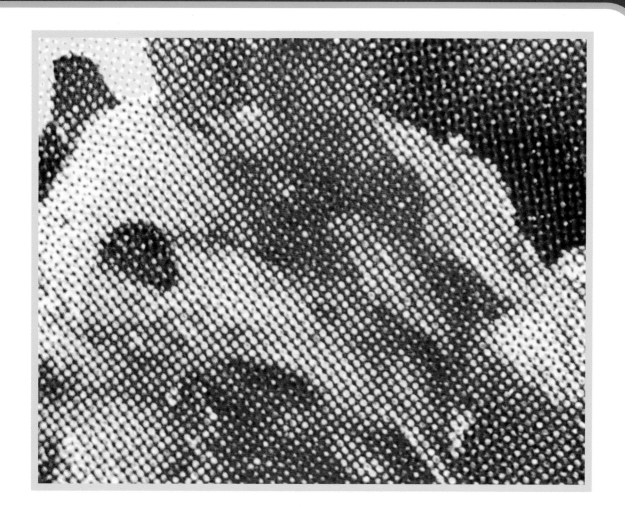

This is what one of the pictures looks like through a **magnifying glass**. Hundreds of small dots of red and yellow make the colour orange.

Coloured lights

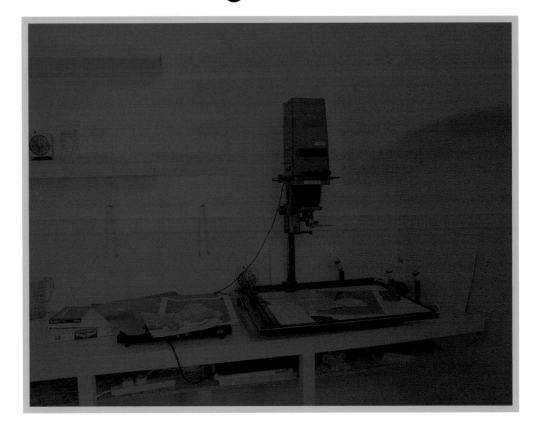

Different coloured lights can change the way we see things. The light in this room is red. It makes everything else look red too!

Theatres use **spotlights** to make patches of different colours. Red and blue lights are shining on this stage.

Mixing coloured light

Mixing coloured light is different to mixing paints. Red and blue lights mixed together give purple. Red and green lights mixed together give yellow.

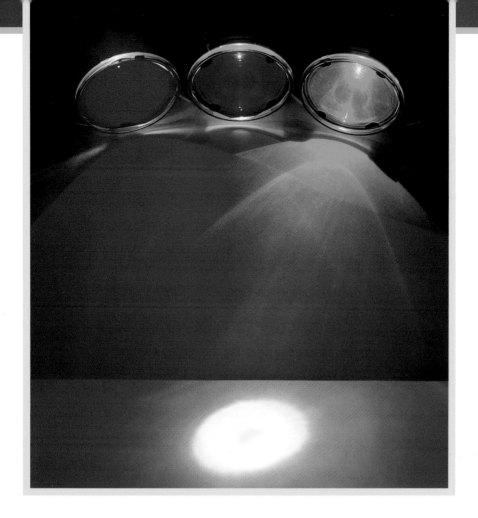

Red, blue and green are **primary** light colours. What happens when you mix red, blue and green lights together?

Colour television

Television and computer screens use tiny squares of coloured light. Using just red, green and blue lights, they make all the different colours.

This is a **magnified** view of a
television screen. It shows how tiny
patches of light mix together to make
different colours.

Rainbows

When the Sun shines after rain, you often see a rainbow in the sky. The colours are always red, orange, yellow, green, blue, indigo and violet.

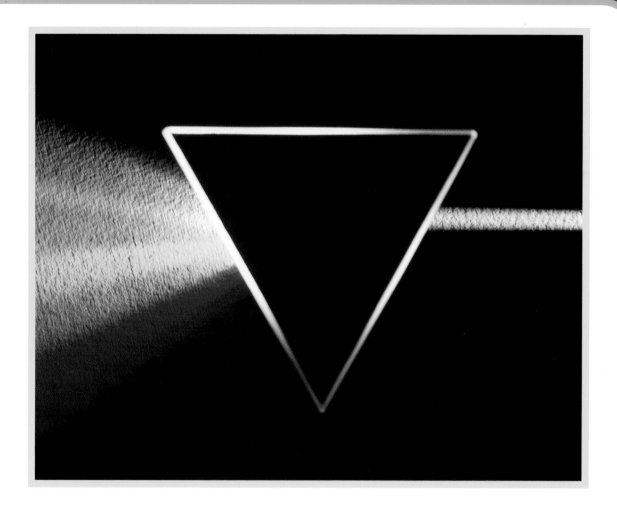

Drops of water in the sky split white
sunlight into different colours, just like
this **prism** does. So white light makes
all the colours of light!

Glossary

charcoal black stick made by partly burning wood

dye substance used to change the colour of cloth, hair and other things

magnified made to look bigger

magnifying glass piece of curved glass that makes things look bigger than they are

pigment any substance used for colouring

primary colour basic colour from which other colours are made

prism block of glass with a square base and sloping sides

spotlight lamp with a strong, narrow beam of light

waste rubbish

Answers

Page 5 – What is colour?
There are eight different colours – yellow, green, orange, pink, purple, black, white and blue.

Page 11 – Primary colours
The girl is wearing red socks and a red hairband.

Page 18 – Shades of colour
The sponge on the left and the nail varnish on the right are the palest pink.

Page 25 – Mixing coloured light
You get white light when you mix red, blue and green lights together.

Index